PUZZLING QUESTIONS

Delegate's Workbook

A six-week course to explore life's deeper issues

Paul Griffiths
& Martin Robinson

D1514001

MONARCH
BOOKS

Oxford, UK & Grand Rapids, Michigan, USA

First published in the UK in 2012 by Monarch Books
(a publishing imprint of Lion Hudson plc)
Wilkinson House, Jordan Hill Road, Oxford OX2 8DR, England
Tel: +44 (0)1865 302750 Fax: +44 (0)1865 302757
Email: monarch@lionhudson.com
www.lionhudson.com

ISBN 978 1 85424 951 7 (single copy)
ISBN 978 1 85424 952 4 (pack of five)

Distributed by:
UK: Marston Book Services, PO Box 269, Abingdon, Oxon, OX14 4YN
USA: Kregel Publications, PO Box 2607, Grand Rapids, Michigan 49501

The text paper used in this book has been made from wood independently certified as having come from sustainable forests.

British Library Cataloguing Data
A catalogue record for this book is available from the British Library.

Printed and bound in Great Britain by Clays Ltd, St Ives plc

Illustrator: Stephen Lewis

Feedback

Let us know what you thought about the Puzzling Questions course and help us to better understand the questions that people are asking today.

Go to the PQ website and click on the link to our "What people say" survey.

www.puzzlingquestions.org.uk

Contents

Session 3

What happens after I die? 52

Session 4

How can I be happy? 69

Session 5

Why is there suffering in the world? 89

Session 6

What is the spiritual world and how does it impact my life?   111

Introduction

Welcome to Puzzling Questions

The aim of this course is to create some quality space to allow you to explore some of life's deeper questions, reflect on some of the spiritual issues that concern you, and meet other people who are on a spiritual journey themselves.

The course

Puzzling Questions (PQ) is a six-session course that looks at the questions of our identity, what God is like, death and beyond, happiness, suffering, and what it means to be spiritual today.

It has been run in a number of venues around the country and is ideal for those who are wanting to explore life's important questions.

Format

As part of each PQ session you will have the opportunity to meet with others who are on their own spiritual journey, listen to various individuals offering their reflection on that session's question, and then take part in a discussion group based on the session's theme.

What is important is that you feel at home on the course and take the opportunity to either sit back and listen or sit forward and engage fully in the conversations.

How to get the best out of the course

It is really important to try to attend as many of the sessions as you can. Although they each work as an independent unit, if you are able to be at all of them the benefit will be far greater.

To accompany the course we have written a book entitled *How Can I Be Happy? (And Other Conundrums)*, which is available from the Puzzling Questions website (www.puzzlingquestions.org.uk). The book expands further many of the topics that will be raised during the course and can be useful for either preparing for the next session or taking time to reflect on the last session.

Enjoy yourself

Life is far too short to waste the moments and opportunities that we are presented with. Many people have found this course to be incredibly helpful in working out what they think about life's deeper questions, and it has set them on a pathway to further discovery.

This is our hope for you.

How to use this workbook

This workbook has been written to enable you to get the best out of the PQ course.

There is a mix of material in the workbook:

- **Material that explores each of the six PQ sessions**
  In each of the six sessions there will be an introduction to the topic, a list of questions that will be explored at the PQ session, and different items that aim to help you explore the topic in more depth. These additional items include a graffiti wall, someone's personal story of how this question relates to their life, and a list of spiritual exercises for those who want to do something and not just spend their time talking. We are delighted that in each session there is also a poem written by Stewart Henderson.

- **A short description of spiritual practices**
  We are aware that many people are interested in having a go at experiencing God rather than just talking about him or exploring the questions that they have. For those who want to consider engaging with God we have included a short section on spiritual practices. If you decide to give these a try we suggest that you talk with the hosts at your PQ venue or those you meet on the PQ course.

- **A journal**
  Some people find it helpful to compose their thoughts on paper or to record what they think or feel as they go through the PQ course. For this reason we have included in this workbook a spiritual journal section. More information about how to use the journal can be found below.

Top tips for using the workbook

- Fill in as much or as little of the workbook as you want to and bring it along with you to the PQ sessions.

- Write all over the workbook, marking with an "x" the bits you disagree with, marking with a "?" the bits you are unsure of, and marking with a "✓" the bits you agree with.

- Use the workbook to think back over the questions you looked at in the last session.

- Use the workbook to think about the questions you will look at in the next session.

- Use the workbook to go deeper into the topic of each session.

Keeping a journal

Some people might find it helpful to keep a spiritual journal as they take part in a Puzzling Questions course. For those who do, we have included the following section in your workbook.

You do not have to journal to be part of the course. It is an optional extra that many people enjoy using.

What is a spiritual journal?

A journal is like a spiritual scrapbook or diary. It gives you an opportunity to reflect on your day spiritually. It provides a moment to take a breath and think about what you have seen, experienced, and encountered over the last little while.

This journal is yours. What you do with it is up to you. You can keep it private or let others read your scribbles.

It is an opportunity to record your journey over the six weeks that you are doing Puzzling Questions.

Our hope is that this journal will be a place for reflection on how God appears in your life – a place you will return to.

Why journal?

There are many reasons why people keep a journal. Some take up journalling because it helps them to express the thoughts and feelings that they have. Other people journal because it forms a record of their time with Puzzling Questions that they can revisit at a later date.

How to keep a journal

Many people journal every day. That doesn't mean that you can't take a break from it and then come back to it.

The best way of journalling is to find a time of day when you can take fifteen minutes for yourself.

As we outline below, there are three sections to each page of the journal. It is up to you how many of the sections you fill in.

Journal sections

a. What's on your mind

What you write in this section is really up to you. If you want you can use the journal to write down what you feel about things. If you want to write so much that you fill the whole section then go ahead, or if you want to put just one word then that's fine too. If you prefer to draw or doodle rather than write, again the decision is yours.

As for what you could write about in this section, we offer the following suggestions:

Observations – make a note of one particular thing that you have sensed or observed since you last journalled.

Reflections – have you been thinking about something recently?

Insights – is there a piece of wisdom that you have gained over the last couple of days?

Prayers – an opportunity to write a prayer that you feel has formed inside you or that you are keen to give to God.

Words of others – a piece of wisdom that you picked up from reading or while talking to someone or watching a film.

Surprises – has something happened that took you by surprise?

Questions – are there questions that you are asking yourself?

Difficulties – what are you wrestling with?

Hopes – is there a dream that you have or a hope for a particular situation?

Things you are thankful for – what good stuff has been going on lately?

b. Stuff to mull over

Take a look at the Bible passage for the week and ask yourself some of the following questions:

- What does the text tell me about God?
- What does the passage tell me about me?
- What does the passage tell me about the world I live in?
- Is there an instruction to be worked out?
- Are there any other spiritual comments in this passage?

The Bible sections are listed on each of the journal pages.

c. God talk

This is an opportunity to talk to God about what you have written in the "What's on your mind" section or read and thought about in the "Stuff to mull over" section.

For those who would prefer to use the words of others, we suggest that you recite the Lord's Prayer and say it over your day and thoughts. You might find that it prompts ideas and thoughts in your mind that you could chat to God about. A copy of the Lord's Prayer is found on page 138.

Session 1:
Who am I?

Introduction

Some recent research conducted by Coventry Cathedral, which investigated the spiritual questions that people are asking, suggests that identity is a huge issue for a good percentage of the population.

The core question of identity goes far beyond the information that may be contained on an identity card – our name, date of birth, address, and national insurance number. Even a reflection on our life story fails to give immediate answers to the troubling question of who the real "us" actually is. Some would suggest that it is the failure to resolve this issue that leads to the proverbial mid-life crisis: the moment that comes when we have achieved the basics in life – a home, a family, a job, a circle of friends – and yet still something eludes us.

The basic question of human identity can be approached from a number of perspectives. From the perspective of biology we are all 70 per cent water and 18 per cent carbon (a similar kind to pencil lead!), with additional percentages of calcium (chalk), and iron. We can be categorized as *Homo sapiens*, a species which has evolved over eons, part of a particular branch of animals with a complex history that includes earlier human species that did not survive.

From the perspective of social history we are also part of a human story that gives rise to a particular struggle and narrative that helps to give identity to the nation in which we live. In contemporary society we are also viewed as "customers" who further define personal identity by means of the products we buy, the clothes we wear, and the lifestyle we develop.

But none of these aspects addresses the deeper question of the uniqueness that comprises us. At one level this is a profoundly spiritual question, and even if we do not see ourselves as "religious people" with particular faith commitments, we don't have to avoid spiritual questions just because they might be unfamiliar to us in our everyday conversations.

Discussion questions

What three words would your friends use to describe you?

How do people define their identity today? Why?

What do you think about that?

How do people lose their sense of identity?

What do you think of the idea that the fashion industry can be an expression of our spiritual DNA – that we are creative people?

What other forms of creativity are expressions of our divine DNA?

Do you see yourself as a spiritual being?

Does physical beauty equal happiness? Why/why not?

How free are we to become the people we really are inside?

What pressures are we under to conform?

Why do we struggle with what is perceived as "ugly"?

How do we develop the ability to see true beauty?

Have we lost our soul (true identity) in the pursuit of what mainstream culture defines as beautiful?

When do you encounter beauty?

   How does it make you feel?

   Why?

What does it mean to be human?

Graffiti – Who am I?

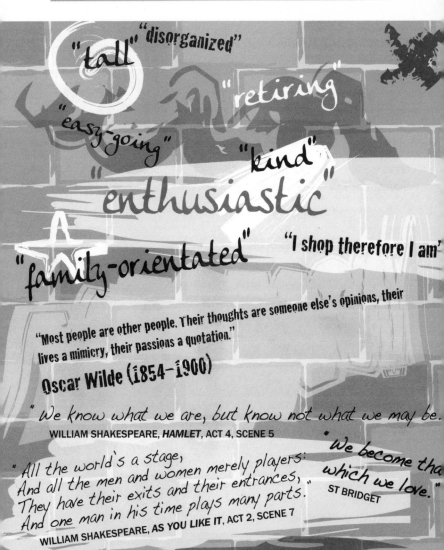

"tall" "disorganized"

"retiring"

"easy-going"

"kind"

"enthusiastic"

"family-orientated"

"I shop therefore I am"

"Most people are other people. Their thoughts are someone else's opinions, their lives a mimicry, their passions a quotation."

Oscar Wilde (1854–1900)

"We know what we are, but know not what we may be."
WILLIAM SHAKESPEARE, *HAMLET*, ACT 4, SCENE 5

"All the world's a stage,
And all the men and women merely players:
They have their exits and their entrances,
And one man in his time plays many parts."
WILLIAM SHAKESPEARE, *AS YOU LIKE IT*, ACT 2, SCENE 7

"We become that which we love."
ST BRIDGET

"Our achievements of today are but the sum total of our thoughts of yesterday. You are today where the thoughts of yesterday have brought you and you will be tomorrow where the thoughts of today take you."
BLAISE PASCAL (1623–62)

Guess who?[1]

1. Which British political advisor famously said, "We don't do God"?

2. By those who stand on the terraces of Liverpool Football Club he is known as God. Who is he?

3. Whose official biography is entitled *Rabble-rouser for Peace*?

4. She is reputed to have introduced punk and the new wave into mainstream fashion. She also made the wedding dress worn by Carrie Bradshaw in the film *Sex and the City*. Who is she?

5. With whom in 1869 did the story of DNA recognition begin?

6. Who said, "The medium is the message"?

7. He played the President's Chief of Staff in *The American President* and later went on to play the President in the drama *The West Wing*, which lasted for seven seasons. Who is he?

8. Famous Welsh actress from Swansea.

9. A leading British women's rights activist born in 1858 in Manchester, she founded the Women's Franchise League and helped found the Women's Social and Political Union. Who was she?

10. Who famously said, *"Cogito ergo sum"*?

---

1   The answers to "Guess who?" can be found on p. 140.

COLUMBO COULDN'T GET ME

Columbo couldn't get me;
the same goes for Poirot.
Sherlock Holmes is baffled;
Rebus doesn't know.

Wallander is silent;
Miss Marple's not inspired.
The case remains a mystery
now that Frost's retired.

My enquiry is specific,
though as endless as the sky,
so I quizzed a passing Time Lord,
asking, "Doctor... who... am I?"

He offered complex theories
which mangled up my head –
unlike his sonic screwdriver,
I couldn't find a thread.

So where to go for answers
with such little progress made,
as I line up and inspect
my own identity parade?

STEWART HENDERSON

When you look in the mirror, what do you see?

If you are made in the image of God, what do you think that means for you?

Mandy's story...

I had been married for thirteen years when my husband told me that he didn't love me any more and had met someone else. He eventually left me and my three daughters to be with his new partner. It was probably the most painful experience of my life. I loved being a wife and a mother; my whole identity had been defined by those roles. Suddenly I was no longer who I thought I was, and I didn't even recognize myself.

I had been a stay-at-home mum ever since I was pregnant with my first daughter. I knew who I was as a mother, and I knew who I was as a wife. But now I looked in the mirror and didn't recognize the face staring back at me... who was this woman?

My identity crisis came to a head when my daughters and I went to visit my sister in Washington, DC, for Christmas. We'd been Christmas shopping in big American malls, visiting museums, and looking at all the fabulous American Christmas decorations, and then one evening after dinner my sister turned to me and said, "Mand, we've been doing lots of things the girls want to do; what would *you* like to do?" I just looked at her dumbfounded, because I had absolutely no idea what I enjoyed doing any more. It was a rude awakening and I realized that I needed to rediscover myself and even discover things about myself that I might not even have known before.

I had been a Christian since my early twenties and had a strong faith in God, but during the period of my separation and divorce what had just been a faith became far more.

The Bible became very important to me during that time; when I was hurting or sad I would read it; I didn't understand it all – in fact I understood very little – but some of it was so beautiful that it became like a healing balm to my aching heart. As I read the Bible more, I discovered something I hadn't realized before: I began to discover lots of descriptions that God uses about us, and they were overwhelming. I read that God saw me as a princess; he saw me as beautiful. When your husband leaves you for another woman, you feel fat and ugly; you certainly don't feel very beautiful! I read that I was fearfully and wonderfully made, that I was loved with an overwhelming, unconditional, everlasting love – and that was amazing to me, because I felt so very unlovable. I read that I'd been chosen, that I was unique and special, that there was no one like me, and these were just a few of the descriptions I discovered.

As I read these descriptions of how God saw me, I made a conscious choice to start believing them. It sounds a lot easier than it actually was, but, when I felt at my most fat and ugly, I would tell myself that God saw me as beautiful, and something wonderful then began to take place. I started to believe it, and as I started to believe that I was beautiful and loved I started to discover who I was and who I was meant to be. I gained more confidence, I began to discover things that made me happy, and I began to go out more with my friends. I rediscovered music – I adore music; I'd forgotten that – and one of the loveliest things that happened was that I started to laugh again... I love laughing!

I discovered that God wants us to find out who we were created to be: the Bible says we were created in his image, so it's a pretty amazing image to resemble. I don't ever want to go back to being the woman I was before my marriage broke up. I have lost so much, but gained so much more. I honestly like myself now, and when anyone asks me the question "What would you like to do?" I know what I'd like to do, and more often than not it involves friends, chocolate, and a lot of laughter!

Spiritual exercises

1. Treat yourself and a friend to a coffee/drink in a very public place and watch the world go by. What do you see?

2. Visit your local museum. What does it tell you about your identity?

3. Describe yourself in three words.

4. Read a typical glossy magazine. What is the relationship between the magazine and what the Bible has to say about who we are?

Rummaging around in the Bible: Psalm 139

Two of the attributes of God are that he is all-knowing and everywhere – the technical words for these are omniscient (all-knowing) and omnipresent (everywhere).

In Psalm 139, its author, David, muses over the fact that he cannot hide from God:

*O Lord, you have searched me
and you know me.
You know when I sit and when I rise;
you perceive my thoughts from afar.
You discern my going out and my lying down;
you are familiar with all my ways.
Before a word is on my tongue
you know it completely, O Lord.*

*You hem me in – behind and before;
you have laid your hand upon me.
Such knowledge is too wonderful for me,
too lofty for me to attain.*

*Where can I go from your Spirit?
Where can I flee from your presence?
If I go up to the heavens, you are there;
if I make my bed in the depths, you are there.
If I rise on the wings of the dawn,
if I settle on the far side of the sea,
even there your hand will guide me,
your right hand will hold me fast.*

*If I say, "Surely the darkness will hide me
and the light become night around me,"
even the darkness will not be dark to you;
the night will shine like the day,
for darkness is as light to you.*

For you created my inmost being;

you knit me together in my mother's womb.
I praise you because I am fearfully and wonderfully made;
your works are wonderful,
I know that full well.
My frame was not hidden from you
when I was made in the secret place.
When I was woven together in the depths of the earth,
your eyes saw my unformed body.
All the days ordained for me
were written in your book
before one of them came to be.

How precious to me are your thoughts, O God!
How vast is the sum of them!
Were I to count them,
they would outnumber the grains of sand.
When I awake, I am still with you.

If only you would slay the wicked, O God!
Away from me, you bloodthirsty men!
They speak of you with evil intent;
your adversaries misuse your name.
Do I not hate those who hate you, O Lord,

and abhor those who rise up against you?
I have nothing but hatred for them;
I count them my enemies.

Search me, O God, and know my heart;
test me and know my anxious thoughts.
See if there is any offensive way in me,
and lead me in the way everlasting.

Q. Reflecting on Psalm 139, what can be said about what it means to be human?

Q. The psalmist defines his life through his dealings with God; what do you think about that?

That's interesting!

For the writers of the Bible the question of our identity is always answered in the context that there is a God.

Thought for the day

Do the brands we buy define who we are?

DAY 1
Journal... personal reactions to spiritual matters

What's on your mind... observations, reflections, insights, prayers, words of others, surprises, questions, trials, yearnings, and things to be thankful for.

Stuff to mull over – take a look at the passage for the week, which is **Psalm 139:1–24** (pages 24–25), and ask yourself the following: What does the passage say about God, me, others, the world I live in, life... anything else?

God talk – time to talk to God about what you have read and written or to read the Lord's Prayer. Try to say it over your day. Is there anything you particularly want to say to God?

DAY 2
Journal... personal reactions to spiritual matters

What's on your mind... observations, reflections, insights, prayers, words of others, surprises, questions, trials, yearnings, and things to be thankful for.

_____

_____

_____

_____

Stuff to mull over – take a look at the passage for the week, which is **Psalm 139:1–24**, and ask yourself the following: What does the passage say about God, me, others, the world I live in, life... anything else?

_____

_____

_____

_____

God talk – time to talk to God about what you have read and written or to read the Lord's Prayer. Try to say it over your day. Is there anything you particularly want to say to God?

_____

_____

_____

_____

DAY 3

Journal... personal reactions to spiritual matters

What's on your mind... observations, reflections, insights, prayers, words of others, surprises, questions, trials, yearnings, and things to be thankful for.

_____

_____

_____

_____

Stuff to mull over – take a look at the passage for the week, which is **Psalm 139:1–24**, and ask yourself the following: What does the passage say about God, me, others, the world I live in, life... anything else?

_____

_____

_____

_____

God talk – time to talk to God about what you have read and written or to read the Lord's Prayer. Try to say it over your day. Is there anything you particularly want to say to God?

_____

_____

_____

_____

DAY 4
Journal... personal reactions to spiritual matters

What's on your mind... observations, reflections, insights, prayers, words of others, surprises, questions, trials, yearnings, and things to be thankful for.

_____

_____

_____

_____

Stuff to mull over – take a look at the passage for the week, which is **Psalm 139:1–24**, and ask yourself the following: What does the passage say about God, me, others, the world I live in, life... anything else?

_____

_____

_____

_____

God talk – time to talk to God about what you have read and written or to read the Lord's Prayer. Try to say it over your day. Is there anything you particularly want to say to God?

_____

_____

_____

_____

DAY 5
Journal... personal reactions to spiritual matters

What's on your mind... observations, reflections, insights, prayers, words of others, surprises, questions, trials, yearnings, and things to be thankful for.

Stuff to mull over – take a look at the passage for the week, which is **Psalm 139:1–24**, and ask yourself the following: What does the passage say about God, me, others, the world I live in, life... anything else?

God talk – time to talk to God about what you have read and written or to read the Lord's Prayer. Try to say it over your day. Is there anything you particularly want to say to God?

DAY 6
Journal... personal reactions to spiritual matters

What's on your mind... observations, reflections, insights, prayers, words of others, surprises, questions, trials, yearnings, and things to be thankful for.

_____

_____

_____

_____

Stuff to mull over – take a look at the passage for the week, which is **Psalm 139:1–24**, and ask yourself the following: What does the passage say about God, me, others, the world I live in, life... anything else?

_____

_____

_____

_____

God talk – time to talk to God about what you have read and written or to read the Lord's Prayer. Try to say it over your day. Is there anything you particularly want to say to God?

_____

_____

_____

_____

DAY 7
Journal... personal reactions to spiritual matters

What's on your mind... observations, reflections, insights, prayers, words of others, surprises, questions, trials, yearnings, and things to be thankful for.

_____

_____

_____

_____

Stuff to mull over – take a look at the passage for the week, which is **Psalm 139:1–24**, and ask yourself the following: What does the passage say about God, me, others, the world I live in, life... anything else?

_____

_____

_____

_____

God talk – time to talk to God about what you have read and written or to read the Lord's Prayer. Try to say it over your day. Is there anything you particularly want to say to God?

_____

_____

_____

_____

Session 2:
What is God like?

Introduction

God is back. This arresting title of a recent book[2] draws attention to the fact that interest in God, faith, and religion in general is rising around the world. Contrary to the twentieth-century European view that religion and God would gradually fade from people's immediate horizon and even memory, the exact reverse has taken place.

However, when we get to the question "What do people believe about God?", the answers become less clear. There seems to be a wide range of ideas about who God is and what he might be like.

Some see God in the traditional Christian framework – God as a loving Father – but many have a much more tentative idea of what the term "God" means. "God" can mean a vague spirit, an invisible force, nature itself (sometimes called Gaia), or simply an unknowable and distant deity impossible to describe.

2   By John Micklethwait and Adrian Wooldridge, London: The Penguin Press, 2009.

Discussion questions

Why do you think God is back in vogue?

Where do people get their ideas of what God is like?

What experiences or events have helped you form your ideas about God?

If God is everywhere, where do you see him?

How do you think people can connect with God?

What do you think of the idea that God cannot be boxed in and is beyond our understanding?

Is it comforting or disturbing?

Do you think viewing God as a father is helpful – a father who cares, loves, smiles?

Jesus claimed that one of his roles was to reveal to people what God was like. At one point he claimed that those who had seen him had seen God. What do you think that means?

What do you think of the idea that Jesus might be the key to understanding God?

In what ways do you think a belief in Jesus/God could be an inconvenience?

Is that a good or a bad thing?

If someone were to encounter God, what would be the right way to respond?

If you have ever had a God encounter, how did you respond?

How does your concept of God compare with the idea of God presented in the Puzzling Questions session?

Graffiti – What is God like?

WHAT WAS BEFORE GOD?

What was before God?
And where did God come from
before God arrived?
And, another thing,
what does God remember about it?

How big is God's memory?
Bigger than China?
Or, like bone china,
which, when you hold it to the light,
all you see is more light
but denser light?

Is God like us?
But needing
a cosmic mantelpiece
full of silver-framed recollections
of planets that he's made?
Or, are we God's memory?
Full of journeys and reminiscences
a reminder that we were... before,
are, and will be?

...So, is it that God looks like us,
but... without the blemishes
...inside and out?

STEWART HENDERSON

Word search

P	N	O	A	P	L	I	M	M	U	T	A	B	L	E	O
T	A	M	E	F	A	I	T	H	F	U	L	D	R	L	T
N	K	H	M	A	D	H	S	P	I	R	I	T	O	P	D
E	O	N	N	T	A	O	B	R	E	C	V	M	T	E	Z
D	M	I	J	H	P	O	K	G	M	U	K	N	A	F	U
N	N	U	Y	E	Z	H	O	L	Y	N	E	D	E	T	F
E	I	U	T	R	G	S	M	I	T	S	Y	I	R	U	O
C	S	M	Y	S	I	K	N	N	E	G	R	A	C	E	R
S	C	O	C	N	E	B	I	R	E	M	C	S	I	W	G
N	I	X	G	O	O	D	P	I	R	D	A	J	N	Z	I
A	E	M	N	B	G	I	O	U	C	S	F	L	Q	J	V
R	N	F	I	T	N	J	T	S	O	T	R	R	Z	J	I
T	T	L	V	M	T	Q	E	T	E	R	N	A	L	T	N
J	Q	X	O	P	I	X	N	E	F	P	T	R	O	S	G
V	K	A	L	O	V	H	T	J	R	G	S	N	V	U	P
A	S	F	C	V	J	D	G	I	E	L	H	T	U	J	W
M	E	R	C	I	F	U	L	O	H	W	B	G	O	K	A

Descriptions of God

Holy – orientated towards what is fun
Omnipotent – all-powerful
Forgiving – doesn't treat us as we deserve
Grace – working for our good
Good – full of life-enriching qualities
Transcendent – beyond our understanding
Father – sees us as his children
Loving – gives himself to us
Eternal – has always been

Merciful – saves us from ourselves
Omniscient – knows everything
Immutable – does not change
Creator – kicked the whole thing off
Faithful – never gives up on us
Just – acts fairly
Omnipresent – can be found everywhere
Spirit – not seen with human eyes

Steve's story...

I think God's likeness can be seen everywhere – my challenge is to open my eyes and look out for it.

I'm very fortunate at the moment to be learning to fly. I've had many lessons, taken many exams, and got my medical cleared, and I went solo for the first time a few weeks ago.

I have never been so scared in all my life. They tell me I was white and unusually quiet as the time approached to start the engine. The weather was good, my instructor was on the radio, yet I was petrified.

I lined up the aircraft, went through my checks, and finally got to the point where I had to push my foot onto the throttle and accelerate down the field.

I don't think I breathed for the few seconds it took for the plane to get to take-off speed, and as the plane lifted off the ground my heart was pounding, and I was full of adrenaline.

For me, I think God is in those exhilarating moments – moments of adventure, and of feeling terrified, moments of sheer excitement.

My God is someone who is up for an adventure – he keeps me company in the ones that I go on, and he often invites me to get involved in some of the things he is doing in this world.

I think God is anything other than dull and boring.

When I landed safely twenty minutes later, I remember taxiing up the runway to the hangar, to be met by applauding pilots and my instructor grinning from ear to ear. I was happy to be back alive too!

As well as learning to fly, I spend some of my time playing the piano... I get a real buzz out of being a musician. It is quite something to be able to sit down and either play through a great piece of music created by someone else or have a go at writing my own.

I believe God gave us the ability to create music and I think that very often it can give us a glimpse of what he is like.

But, you know, the place where I discover what God is like more than anywhere else is in the relationships I have with my parents, my wife, and our children.

My eldest daughter had her birthday last week, and it reminded me of how much I love my kids, and how much I love my wife. Before I became a parent it was difficult to imagine how I would feel, and how strong those feelings could be. Now I am one, I think I've understood a small part of God's character. God not only loves everyone in my family, he also loves me – with an intensity that is greater than any love I could have for my children.

It's not just in family units, though, that God can be understood a little – I was watching a TV fund-raising day a few weeks ago, and found myself moved by the film clips of kids in a third-world country.

Their needs were so great; life was so hard for them, and the disease so cruel, that I had to give money to an organization that could make a significant difference. I'm not alone in that, of course, because I know that acts of compassion are demonstrated daily by people all across the world, many of which aren't recognized or put on TV, yet in those moments of compassion and faithfulness I think a bit of God's character can be seen.

Where would you go to find out what God is like?

Does Jesus offer us a clue to discovering what God is like?

Spiritual exercises

1. Go with a friend for a walk to a well-known nearby beauty spot... what does the splendour of nature tell you about what God is like?

2. Go onto Google Earth and spend time exploring the planet.

3. Take a look at Google Earth and explore space, or take a look at the NASA images of space.

4. What can you learn about God from songs in the music charts?

5. Visit a local art gallery and consider the different artists' "take" on God.

6. Google Michelangelo's "Creation of Man" panel from the ceiling of the Sistine Chapel and consider what it tells us about God.

Rummaging around in the Bible: Luke 15:11– 24

The religious leaders of Jesus' day are having a go at him because he is spending so much time with the outcasts of their society.

In the three stories located in Luke chapter 15 (the lost sheep, the lost coin and the one that we are looking at, the lost son), Jesus illustrates to these disenchanted religious folk that the God he is serving not only loves the outcasts of society but goes in search of them.

In Luke 15:11–24 he paints the picture of a father who breaks with social protocol to welcome home his returning repentant son.

Jesus told this story to remind people of what God is like.

The Parable of the Lost Son

Jesus continued: "There was a man who had two sons. The younger one said to his father, 'Father, give me my share of the estate.' So he divided his property between them.

"Not long after that, the younger son got together all he had, set off for a distant country and there squandered his wealth in wild living. After he had spent everything, there was a severe famine in that whole country, and he began to be in need. So he went and hired himself out to a citizen of that country, who sent him to his fields to feed pigs. He longed to fill his stomach with the pods that the pigs were eating, but no one gave him anything.

"When he came to his senses, he said, 'How many of my father's hired men have food to spare, and here I am starving to death! I will set out and go back to my father and say to him: Father, I have sinned against heaven and against you. I am no longer worthy to be called your son; make me like one of your hired men.' So he got up and went to his father.

"But while he was still a long way off, his father saw him and was filled with compassion for him; he ran to his son, threw his arms around him and kissed him.

"The son said to him, 'Father, I have sinned against heaven and against you. I am no longer worthy to be called your son.'

"But the father said to his servants, 'Quick! Bring the best robe and put it on him. Put a ring on his finger and sandals on his feet. Bring the fattened calf and kill it. Let's have a feast and celebrate. For this son of mine was dead and is alive again; he was lost and is found.' So they began to celebrate."

Q. What can we discover about God from this story (assuming the father in the story represents God)?

That's interesting!

The Bible does not try to prove the existence of God – it takes it for granted.

DAY 8
Journal... personal reactions to spiritual matters

What's on your mind... observations, reflections, insights, prayers, words of others, surprises, questions, trials, yearnings, and things to be thankful for.

Stuff to mull over – take a look at the passage for the week, which is **Luke 15:11–24** (pages 43–44), and ask yourself the following: What does the passage say about God, me, others, the world I live in, life... anything else?

God talk – time to talk to God about what you have read and written or to read the Lord's Prayer. Try to say it over your day. Is there anything you particularly want to say to God?

DAY 9

Journal... personal reactions to spiritual matters

What's on your mind... observations, reflections, insights, prayers, words of others, surprises, questions, trials, yearnings, and things to be thankful for.

_____

_____

_____

_____

Stuff to mull over – take a look at the passage for the week, which is **Luke 15:11–24**, and ask yourself the following: What does the passage say about God, me, others, the world I live in, life... anything else?

_____

_____

_____

_____

God talk – time to talk to God about what you have read and written or to read the Lord's Prayer. Try to say it over your day. Is there anything you particularly want to say to God?

_____

_____

_____

_____

DAY 10
Journal... personal reactions to spiritual matters

What's on your mind... observations, reflections, insights, prayers, words of others, surprises, questions, trials, yearnings, and things to be thankful for.

Stuff to mull over – take a look at the passage for the week, which is **Luke 15:11–24**, and ask yourself the following: What does the passage say about God, me, others, the world I live in, life... anything else?

God talk – time to talk to God about what you have read and written or to read the Lord's Prayer. Try to say it over your day. Is there anything you particularly want to say to God?

DAY 11

Journal... personal reactions to spiritual matters

What's on your mind... observations, reflections, insights, prayers, words of others, surprises, questions, trials, yearnings, and things to be thankful for.

_____

_____

_____

_____

Stuff to mull over – take a look at the passage for the week, which is **Luke 15:11–24**, and ask yourself the following: What does the passage say about God, me, others, the world I live in, life... anything else?

_____

_____

_____

_____

God talk – time to talk to God about what you have read and written or to read the Lord's Prayer. Try to say it over your day. Is there anything you particularly want to say to God?

_____

_____

_____

_____

DAY 12
Journal... personal reactions to spiritual matters

What's on your mind... observations, reflections, insights, prayers, words of others, surprises, questions, trials, yearnings, and things to be thankful for.

_____

_____

_____

_____

Stuff to mull over – take a look at the passage for the week, which is **Luke 15:11–24**, and ask yourself the following: What does the passage say about God, me, others, the world I live in, life... anything else?

_____

_____

_____

_____

God talk – time to talk to God about what you have read and written or to read the Lord's Prayer. Try to say it over your day. Is there anything you particularly want to say to God?

_____

_____

_____

DAY 13
Journal... personal reactions to spiritual matters

What's on your mind... observations, reflections, insights, prayers, words of others, surprises, questions, trials, yearnings, and things to be thankful for.

_____

_____

_____

_____

Stuff to mull over – take a look at the passage for the week, which is **Luke 15:11–24**, and ask yourself the following: What does the passage say about God, me, others, the world I live in, life... anything else?

_____

_____

_____

_____

God talk – time to talk to God about what you have read and written or to read the Lord's Prayer. Try to say it over your day. Is there anything you particularly want to say to God?

_____

_____

_____

DAY 14

Journal... personal reactions to spiritual matters

What's on your mind... observations, reflections, insights, prayers, words of others, surprises, questions, trials, yearnings, and things to be thankful for.

Stuff to mull over – take a look at the passage for the week, which is **Luke 15:11–24**, and ask yourself the following: What does the passage say about God, me, others, the world I live in, life... anything else?

God talk – time to talk to God about what you have read and written or to read the Lord's Prayer. Try to say it over your day. Is there anything you particularly want to say to God?

Session 3:
What happens after I die?

Introduction

As the epic final part of Tolkien's Lord of the Rings trilogy, *The Return of the King*, draws to a close, we find its leading characters all gathering at the quayside. They are there to say goodbye to those who are about to catch the last ship to leave Middle-earth. It is a scene full of emotion and fond farewells, as those leaving on the ship know they can never return to those they are leaving behind. There is, however, a sense of peace and purpose in their final voyage.

This ship could be seen as representing our last journey here on earth – the idea is that death is our last great adventure as we sail to the world beyond. Death is not seen as the end, but purely a voyage we must all take as we head for that new life beyond the grave.

Discussion questions

If you discovered that you had only a short time to live, what changes would you make to how you live now? What would you do with the time you had left?

What fears do people have about dying and death?

Should having a belief in God make a difference to how you die?

Why do some people feel they need to "put their house in order" before they die?

What happens after death?

If there is a heaven, what do you think it is like? What would make it "heaven" for you?

When should we start thinking about our death?

Would we be a better society if we faced up to the reality that we are all going to die?

Why do we avoid the subject of death?

How ready do you feel to face death?

Have you ever had a near-death experience?

How would you like to be remembered?

Graffiti – What happens after I die?

THE LONG-DECEASED EMPEROR

The long-deceased emperor
in his opulent tomb,
the oligarch
sheltering in his Panic Room.
The charity worker,
the doctor on call,
the nun and the villain –
it comes to us all.

The consultant confirming
that nothing now works...
...no more X-Factor:
mm, death has its perks.
The still undertaker
at Fate's final vow;
the dental appointment
that's not needed now.

The pauper's cremation,
the lying in state,
the elephant's graveyard
where all creatures wait.
The confident atheist
convinced there's no more;
the neutral agnostic
who isn't so sure.

The flamboyant, the shy,
the wastrel or grafter –
all we can say
is we get to hear... after.

STEWART HENDERSON

Gravestones

Humanity has always marked the burial site of its dead. Initially it was with rocks, but as culture developed, the way we marked someone's resting place became more refined.

For some, marking their own death or the death of a loved one can still be a moment to encourage a chuckle!

What would you put on *your* gravestone?

Sue's story...

I have watched many people die over my years nursing – some in hospital, many at home. Some people are clearly frightened when they know the time is approaching, but most slip away quietly in the end, without a fight. And you always know when the moment of death has occurred, because something changes. It's not just that the breathing stops (because sometimes you can hardly hear that anyway), but something intangible, imperceptible, leaves that person. I guess some would suggest that their soul or spirit has left; perhaps you could simply say life has moved on. But it is infinitely clear that the person they were is no longer there.

Many years ago I sat with a man who was terminally ill, and he related to me an earlier near-death experience. He had been crushed by a forklift truck in a work accident many years previously: he told me that he had sincerely believed he was about to die at that moment, and as he was losing consciousness he had seen heaven, and a much-loved dog he once had was waiting for him there. Despite my misgivings at the time about the reality of that experience, it gave him such comfort to know what was waiting for him, now that his life really was about to end, that I couldn't bring myself to challenge what he had seen. And now, many years later, I am glad I didn't, because although I still don't believe our pets meet us after death, my understanding of what happens when we die has changed radically, and I certainly no longer believe I have all the right answers.

I have also talked to spiritualists who have been present at the death of a close family member and who have been absolutely convinced that they have seen deceased relatives gathering around the bedside (obviously invisible to everyone else!) as the time approached. This has also made a huge difference to the way they have perceived and accepted death. But, whatever foundation we might believe these experiences do or don't have in reality, it still doesn't actually tell us what happens next.

My own father was an atheist through and through, and very much believed that if you couldn't see it, it wasn't real. As I became a Christian when I was seventeen, we had many "lively debates" on what happens after death. Despite my very best (though woefully inadequate) efforts to convince him otherwise, he remained resolutely set against the idea of life after death and firmly believed that there was simply nothing to follow.

I was part of a church in which people had a clearly defined idea of what happened after death, so I was understandably worried about what would happen to my dad when he died. As far as I am aware he remained an atheist up to the very moment he died, which happened very suddenly as he was hit by a motorcyclist one afternoon while crossing a road. I believe he died without ever getting a personal connection with God for himself, and I expected to be devastated by that – but I wasn't.

And that's because I know in the deepest parts of my mind and heart that we have a God who is love. A God who has far more mercy, far more compassion than we can ever understand – a God who knows every single thing about us – understands every thought of our heart ... and yet still loves us. A God who knows and understands and loves my dad better than I ever could, and to whom I can trust his life and death.

Spiritual exercises

1. Take a friend and go to visit a cemetery: look at the gravestones and observe what is written on them... how does a belief in the afterlife affect what was written?

2. During the week, take a look at some obituaries in the local or national press. What do they have to say about what happens after we die?

3. Take a few moments during the week to reflect on how contemporary society views death.

4. Listen to "Imagine" by John Lennon[3] and consider what impact the lyrics of that song would have on your life if the words were true – that there was no heaven.

---

3 "Imagine" is the opening track on his album *Imagine*, released in 1971.

Rummaging around in the Bible: Revelation 21:1-4

A recent game show asked its contestants the question "What do you expect to see in heaven?"

Although the players did their best to answer the question, it was obvious that most of them were unsure of what heaven was like.

In Revelation 21:1-4 we are given a glimpse of what we can expect heaven to be like. To say the least, it should be an amazing place.

The New Jerusalem

Then I saw a new heaven and a new earth, for the first heaven and the first earth had passed away, and there was no longer any sea. I saw the Holy City, the new Jerusalem, coming down out of heaven from God, prepared as a bride beautifully dressed for her husband. And I heard a loud voice from the throne saying, "Now the dwelling of God is with men, and he will live with them. They will be his people, and God himself will be with them and be their God. He will wipe every tear from their eyes. There will be no more death or mourning or crying or pain, for the old order of things has passed away."

Q. What is your picture of heaven?

That's interesting!

Jesus offers little detail when he speaks about eternity or heaven. But he is very clear that heaven is our destination, should we desire it.

The comedian and film director Woody Allen once said, "I'm not afraid of dying; I just don't want to be there when it happens."

DAY 15
Journal... personal reactions to spiritual matters

What's on your mind... observations, reflections, insights, prayers, words of others, surprises, questions, trials, yearnings, and things to be thankful for.

_____

_____

_____

_____

Stuff to mull over – take a look at the passage for the week, which is **Revelation 21:1–4** (page 61), and ask yourself the following: What does the passage say about God, me, others, the world I live in, life... anything else?

_____

_____

_____

_____

God talk – time to talk to God about what you have read and written or to read the Lord's Prayer. Try to say it over your day. Is there anything you particularly want to say to God?

_____

_____

_____

_____

DAY 16
Journal... personal reactions to spiritual matters

What's on your mind... observations, reflections, insights, prayers, words of others, surprises, questions, trials, yearnings, and things to be thankful for.

_____

_____

_____

_____

Stuff to mull over – take a look at the passage for the week, which is **Revelation 21:1–4**, and ask yourself the following: What does the passage say about God, me, others, the world I live in, life... anything else?

_____

_____

_____

_____

God talk – time to talk to God about what you have read and written or to read the Lord's Prayer. Try to say it over your day. Is there anything you particularly want to say to God?

_____

_____

_____

_____

DAY 17
Journal... personal reactions to spiritual matters

What's on your mind... observations, reflections, insights, prayers, words of others, surprises, questions, trials, yearnings, and things to be thankful for.

Stuff to mull over – take a look at the passage for the week, which is **Revelation 21:1–4**, and ask yourself the following: What does the passage say about God, me, others, the world I live in, life... anything else?

God talk – time to talk to God about what you have read and written or to read the Lord's Prayer. Try to say it over your day. Is there anything you particularly want to say to God?

DAY 18
Journal... personal reactions to spiritual matters

What's on your mind... observations, reflections, insights, prayers, words of others, surprises, questions, trials, yearnings, and things to be thankful for.

_____

_____

_____

_____

Stuff to mull over – take a look at the passage for the week, which is **Revelation 21:1–4**, and ask yourself the following: What does the passage say about God, me, others, the world I live in, life... anything else?

_____

_____

_____

_____

God talk – time to talk to God about what you have read and written or to read the Lord's Prayer. Try to say it over your day. Is there anything you particularly want to say to God?

_____

_____

_____

_____

DAY 19
Journal... personal reactions to spiritual matters

What's on your mind... observations, reflections, insights, prayers, words of others, surprises, questions, trials, yearnings, and things to be thankful for.

_____

_____

_____

_____

Stuff to mull over – take a look at the passage for the week, which is **Revelation 21:1–4**, and ask yourself the following: What does the passage say about God, me, others, the world I live in, life... anything else?

_____

_____

_____

_____

God talk – time to talk to God about what you have read and written or to read the Lord's Prayer. Try to say it over your day. Is there anything you particularly want to say to God?

_____

_____

_____

_____

DAY 20
Journal... personal reactions to spiritual matters

What's on your mind... observations, reflections, insights, prayers, words of others, surprises, questions, trials, yearnings, and things to be thankful for.

_____

_____

_____

_____

Stuff to mull over – take a look at the passage for the week, which is **Revelation 21:1–4**, and ask yourself the following: What does the passage say about God, me, others, the world I live in, life... anything else?

_____

_____

_____

_____

God talk – time to talk to God about what you have read and written or to read the Lord's Prayer. Try to say it over your day. Is there anything you particularly want to say to God?

_____

_____

_____

_____

DAY 21
Journal... personal reactions to spiritual matters

What's on your mind... observations, reflections, insights, prayers, words of others, surprises, questions, trials, yearnings, and things to be thankful for.

_____

_____

_____

_____

Stuff to mull over – take a look at the passage for the week, which is **Revelation 21:1–4**, and ask yourself the following: What does the passage say about God, me, others, the world I live in, life... anything else?

_____

_____

_____

_____

God talk – time to talk to God about what you have read and written or to read the Lord's Prayer. Try to say it over your day. Is there anything you particularly want to say to God?

_____

_____

_____

_____

Session 4:
How can I be happy?

Introduction

Our pursuit of happiness is so intense that so far there have been 336 million hits on the search engine Google for this word. With tens of thousands of books in print on this subject, it seems that Aristotle was right when he claimed that happiness is "the ultimate goal of humanity".

None of us want to become obvious candidates for the television programmes *Grumpy Old Men/Women!*[4] With the DNA of a party-pooper, the people on those are similar in outlook to the two Muppets who sat on the balcony during every show expressing nothing but sarcasm and misery.

When we begin to reflect on the positive contribution that happiness makes to our lives, it is no wonder that people have an innate desire to live well. Happiness is an extremely powerful commodity. Recent scientific research informs us that happy people live longer than sad ones. Happy people more often than not have better mental health. Happy people are physically more resilient to illness than sad people. Happy people perform better and, it seems, have an all-round better quality of life.

In the happiness field, three connected questions assume importance. First, what *is* happiness? Second, what is it that makes people happy? Third, is it possible to be happy even when life is difficult?

---

4   BBC2, 2003–present, produced by Liberty Bell TV.

Discussion questions

The philosopher Aristotle claimed that the ultimate goal of humanity is to be happy. Do you think he was right? Why?

Does having more and more "stuff" make people happy?

Is acceptance (of self, of situations, by others) one of the keys to happiness?

Why is comedy (e.g. stand-up, comedy programmes on TV) so popular today?

What makes you laugh?

How important is shared laughter?

Is there a healing element to laughter?

Describe what a happy life would look like for you.

Who is the happiest person you know?

What is your formula for happiness?

Is there a link between God and personal happiness?

Is it possible to be happy when life is difficult?

Graffiti – What makes you happy?

"money in your pocket"

"sunshine"

"getting to where you want to get to"

"good health"

"becoming a dad recently"

"being surrounded by people who love you"

"contentment"

"IF I KNEW THAT, I WOULD BE HAPPY ALL THE TIME"

"good cars, fast women"

"holidays"

"the lunch I have just had"

Quiz

1. Can you name Snow Patrol's "happy" song?

2. A colourful singer, this female artist told us that there was still a long way to go to find happy. Do you know her name?

3. This TV show ran for over ten years. Featuring a character called the Fonz, the name of the show is also the name of this upbeat song. Name that tune!

4. He was everything she ever wanted and yet this rock diva didn't get the happy ending she so dreamed of. Can you name the singer of this 2004 hit?

5. Who had a hit in 1988 with the song "Don't worry, be happy"?

6. After losing their religion, this American rock band got together with the Muppets to sing a remix of their happy song. Name the remix.

7. R. Kelly told us that it not only kept the world moving but it also got us dancing. What was it that did all this? It was also the name of his 2004 hit.

8. With Whoopi Goldberg it is always a happy day. Name the sequel.

9. The Turtles' 1967 hit told us one of the keys to personal happiness. Where did they tell us that happiness could be found?

10. With happy feet this animated lead danced across the silver screen. Who was it?

How can I be happy?

How can I be happy?
What, as in...
the abiding state of pleasure and contentment?

as in... being inhabited by an atmosphere
of dazed delight,
elated with well-being,
jubilant, joyous, and
wearing enormous glitter trousers
that yodel like Tarzan when you sit down...

How can I be happy?...
with a permanent carnival in my heart
and jabberwocky fun fairs in the head.

Can I be happy?...
...with me as my very own helium balloon,
sky high, over the moon, and under the ocean –
arranging starfish
in aquatic constellations of wonder
then...
...being as sunny and as screechy as a chimpanzee
racing through a banana plantation.

How can I be happy?
...as in... as ecstatic as toasted crumpets
awaiting the benediction of butter,
as in... mammoth with merriment,
blissful beaming and giddily glad,
settled with myself,
irrespective of burdens and sorrows by the skipful.

How can we be happy...?
Don't know... Any suggestions?...

STEWART HENDERSON

Charlie Chaplin: A day without laughter is a day wasted!

Sharon's story...

For any *Sex and the City* fans reading this, right now I feel like Carrie Bradshaw about to write her next weekly column! I'm sitting on the bed with my netbook on my lap, thinking about the question "How can I be happy?"

The short, quick answer... eat chocolate and go shopping!

But while chocolate is pure nectar from the gods and shopping is heavenly, they don't really make me happy; they maybe provide an instant fix of happiness but longer term they can produce the opposite, because chocolate just piles on the pounds and shopping spends them!

I don't know if it is possible to come up with an exact formula for happiness, but I can think of occasions when I could say I felt happy.

I was working away once with people I had only met a couple of times. A meal was arranged for a team member who was leaving, and I was invited. Staff who had worked alongside their colleague were sad to see him leave and there was quite a bit of emotion in the room after the farewell speeches, and yet there was something about the evening that made me feel happy. There was a fair amount of hilarity as people performed their party tricks and told jokes, but that in itself did not make me feel happy. There was good food and wine, conversation and dancing, all of which were enjoyable, but I'm still not sure that they were the ingredients that induced a sense of happiness.

So what did make me feel happy?

In a hectic lifestyle with all its stresses and responsibilities, I was able to switch off from the daily grind. I found I was comfortable with the environment I was in; I was comfortable with the people around me and had a sense of connection with them. Most importantly, I felt comfortable with who I was; I was able to be me.

It was in essence a fun evening, but not only did it make me feel happy for the duration of the leaving party (before my head crashed down on the pillow late that night!), but the feeling lingered for the next few days. Somehow the experience of that evening spurred me on once again to look at life more positively and a little differently; it gave me an inner confidence that stayed with me. When the pressures of life start to crowd in, that feeling of happiness can wane, but I have always found that an evening with friends who accept me, where we can laugh together and where I can feel secure enough to accept who I am, makes me feel happy.

I get the same feeling when I am in a village in Africa and spend time with children who have very little, yet exude happiness. On the surface the picture painted is a scene of poverty and despair: having no sanitation or clean drinking water is not something I particularly relish, yet I feel happy. I feel I can be myself; I am with people who accept me for who I am; despite the lack of decent toilet facilities and hot running water, I feel comfortable in my environment.

Acceptance is the biggest factor when it comes to my happiness. Life has not turned out in the way that I thought it would have to in order for me to be happy. When I was a small girl playing with my dolls in the dressing-up corner I imagined my adult life very differently. Although it is not at all easy to accept the things I cannot change, and that can be the big life stuff or just the fact that the scales say something I don't like, it is an ingredient that for me is vital in the recipe for being happy.

So how can I be happy? I guess it's about embracing life, accepting the things I cannot change, spending time with friends, laughing a lot, worrying less, and eating a bit of chocolate and doing a bit of shopping along the way!

The A to Z of gratitude

There is enormous benefit in counting your blessings. Attempt to find something you can be grateful for beginning with each letter of the alphabet:

a

b

c

d

e

f

g

h

i

j

k

l

m

n

o

p

q

r

s

t

u

v

w

x

y

z

Spiritual exercises

1. Counting – take a moment each day this week to identify three things that you can be thankful for.

2. Remembering – at some point during the week, make some time to remember one of the best experiences that you have ever had – with family, with friends or when on holiday.

3. Having conversations – meet up with some friends and take time to catch up and tell stories.

4. Being grateful – attempt to go through the week saying "thank you" to everyone who does you a good turn.

5. Reflecting – watch the film *The Pursuit of Happyness*.[5] Do you agree with the message that the film is presenting?

---

5   2006, director Gabriele Muccino.

Rummaging around in the Bible: Ecclesiastes 2:1–11

Solomon had it all. There was nothing that he went without, and yet despite having everything that you and I might dream of, he still felt that there was something missing.

In his autobiography he tells the story of how he went in search of a life worth living. What we find in Ecclesiastes 2:1–11 is his summary of what he tried and the initial conclusions he came to.

Ecclesiastes 2:1–11

I thought in my heart, "Come now, I will test you with pleasure to find out what is good." But that also proved to be meaningless. "Laughter," I said, "is foolish. And what does pleasure accomplish?" I tried cheering myself with wine, and embracing folly – my mind still guiding me with wisdom. I wanted to see what was worth while for men to do under heaven during the few days of their lives.

I undertook great projects: I built houses for myself and planted vineyards. I made gardens and parks and planted all kinds of fruit trees in them. I made reservoirs to water groves of flourishing trees. I bought male and female slaves and had other slaves who were born in my house. I also owned more herds and flocks than anyone in Jerusalem before me. I amassed silver and gold for myself, and the treasure of kings and provinces. I acquired men and women singers, and a harem as well – the delights of the heart of man. I became greater by far than anyone in Jerusalem before me. In all this my wisdom stayed with me.

I denied myself nothing my eyes desired;
I refused my heart no pleasure.
My heart took delight in all my work,
and this was the reward for all my labour.

Yet when I surveyed all that my hands had done
and what I had toiled to achieve,
everything was meaningless, a chasing after the wind;
nothing was gained under the sun.

Q. Solomon said the pursuit of pleasure (money, possessions,
and experiences) does not bring happiness. Do you agree?

That's interesting!

Solomon said that life is best lived by treating it as a party
to which God is invited.

DAY 22
Journal... personal reactions to spiritual matters

What's on your mind...observations, reflections, insights, prayers, words of others, surprises, questions, trials, yearnings, and things to be thankful for.

Stuff to mull over – take a look at the passage for the week, which is **Ecclesiastes 2:1–11** (pages 80–81), and ask yourself the following: What does the passage say about God, me, others, the world I live in, life... anything else?

God talk – time to talk to God about what you have read and written or to read the Lord's Prayer. Try to say it over your day. Is there anything you particularly want to say to God?

DAY 23
Journal... personal reactions to spiritual matters

What's on your mind...observations, reflections, insights, prayers, words of others, surprises, questions, trials, yearnings, and things to be thankful for.

_____

_____

_____

_____

Stuff to mull over – take a look at the passage for the week, which is **Ecclesiastes 2:1–11**, and ask yourself the following: What does the passage say about God, me, others, the world I live in, life... anything else?

_____

_____

_____

_____

God talk – time to talk to God about what you have read and written or to read the Lord's Prayer. Try to say it over your day. Is there anything you particularly want to say to God?

_____

_____

_____

_____

DAY 24
Journal... personal reactions to spiritual matters

What's on your mind...observations, reflections, insights, prayers, words of others, surprises, questions, trials, yearnings, and things to be thankful for.

_____

_____

_____

Stuff to mull over – take a look at the passage for the week, which is **Ecclesiastes 2:1–11**, and ask yourself the following: What does the passage say about God, me, others, the world I live in, life... anything else?

_____

_____

_____

_____

God talk – time to talk to God about what you have read and written or to read the Lord's Prayer. Try to say it over your day. Is there anything you particularly want to say to God?

_____

_____

_____

DAY 25
Journal... personal reactions to spiritual matters

What's on your mind...observations, reflections, insights, prayers, words of others, surprises, questions, trials, yearnings, and things to be thankful for.

Stuff to mull over – take a look at the passage for the week, which is **Ecclesiastes 2:1–11**, and ask yourself the following: What does the passage say about God, me, others, the world I live in, life... anything else?

God talk – time to talk to God about what you have read and written or to read the Lord's Prayer. Try to say it over your day. Is there anything you particularly want to say to God?

DAY 26
Journal... personal reactions to spiritual matters

What's on your mind...observations, reflections, insights, prayers, words of others, surprises, questions, trials, yearnings, and things to be thankful for.

Stuff to mull over – take a look at the passage for the week, which is **Ecclesiastes 2:1–11**, and ask yourself the following: What does the passage say about God, me, others, the world I live in, life... anything else?

God talk – time to talk to God about what you have read and written or to read the Lord's Prayer. Try to say it over your day. Is there anything you particularly want to say to God?

DAY 27
Journal... personal reactions to spiritual matters

What's on your mind...observations, reflections, insights, prayers, words of others, surprises, questions, trials, yearnings, and things to be thankful for.

Stuff to mull over – take a look at the passage for the week, which is **Ecclesiastes 2:1–11**, and ask yourself the following: What does the passage say about God, me, others, the world I live in, life... anything else?

God talk – time to talk to God about what you have read and written or to read the Lord's Prayer. Try to say it over your day. Is there anything you particularly want to say to God?

DAY 28
Journal... personal reactions to spiritual matters

What's on your mind...observations, reflections, insights, prayers, words of others, surprises, questions, trials, yearnings, and things to be thankful for.

_____

_____

_____

_____

Stuff to mull over – take a look at the passage for the week, which is **Ecclesiastes 2:1–11**, and ask yourself the following: What does the passage say about God, me, others, the world I live in, life... anything else?

_____

_____

_____

_____

God talk – time to talk to God about what you have read and written or to read the Lord's Prayer. Try to say it over your day. Is there anything you particularly want to say to God?

_____

_____

_____

_____

Session 5:
Why is there suffering in the world?

Introduction

Some research was undertaken recently on the things that people were most concerned about. Many of those questioned spoke about the personal suffering that they or a close family member had experienced. Others told of their worries about national problems that were affecting their local communities. Some expressed their fear of the impact that global problems with the environment were having and would have on their lives and the lives of their children.

What underlies all these concerns is an acknowledgment that things are not quite right in our world. Why? Why is there suffering in the world? Why do some suffer from serious physical illness and others escape it? Why does this suffering often happen to those who, on the face of it, have lived relatively good lives? Why does bad stuff happen to good people? Why can't you go out safely at night in some areas? Why is society breaking down? Why are there such global problems as poverty, AIDS, and environmental degradation?

When it comes to looking at why there is so much suffering in the world, we are obviously dealing with a very complex set of problems.

Discussion questions

Have you ever felt strongly enough about something to take action? What did you do (march, protest, petition, write a letter)?

What issues attract your attention?

What can we do individually and with others to alleviate suffering in the world?

What do you think of the idea that each of us personally is responsible for part of what is wrong with the world?

What responsibility do we need to take for the suffering that occurs in our world?

Why is there suffering in the world?

Do you think there is a spiritual dimension to the suffering that some people experience?

Where is God when people suffer?

Have you ever experienced God comforting or helping you when things were difficult?

Have you ever learned anything really important through a tough time?

Is it helpful to see ourselves and others as broken people? Why?

Graffiti – Why is there suffering in the world?

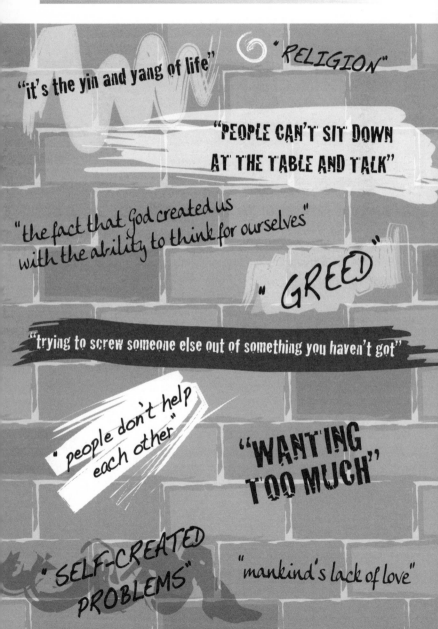

Factoids

1. In 2010, the wealth of Britain's 1,000 richest people rose to £395 billion. And yet, in the fifth-wealthiest country in the world, 1.6 million children live in severe poverty.[6]

2. An independent study by the House of Commons Library showed that incidents of violence against the person increased from 618,417 in 1998 to 887,942 in 2009. That means that violent crime is 44 per cent higher than it was in 1998.[7]

3. Over 1 billion people in the world suffer from hunger, with 100 million being added to the list because of the 2009 global financial crisis.[8] The number of people who went to sleep hungry in the UK in 2010 was in excess of 4 million.[9]

4. Figures show that one in four British adults experience at least one diagnosable mental health problem in any one year, and one in six experience this at any given time.[10]

5. Disabled people are more likely to be unemployed than non-disabled people, and those who are employed are paid less, on average, than non-disabled people.[11]

6. Climate change has been described as the biggest global health challenge of the twenty-first century. If scientists are right then it is likely to affect the health of millions of people across the world. Some of the suggested consequences of a

6 http://www.savethechildren.org.uk/what-we-do/child-poverty/uk-child-poverty
7 http://conservativehome.blogs.com/thetorydiary/2010/03/chris-grayling-vindicated-as-independent-evaluation-concludes-violent-crime-has-risen-by-44-under-la.html
8 http://news.bbc.co.uk/1/hi/8109698.stm
9 http://www.thefoodnetwork.co.uk/Portals/0/docs/FareShare%20-%20SFF.pdf
10 http://www.mentalhealth.org.uk/help-information/mental-health-statistics/UK-worldwide/
11 http://www.shaw-trust.org.uk/facts_and_figures

change in our climate include rising sea levels, heatwaves, floods, and changing patterns in infectious diseases.

7. A human security report published in 2005 noted that the reason for the decline in the number of conflicts in the world was intervention by the United Nations, plus the end of colonialism and the Cold War.[12]

8. In 2011 experts suggested that there were far more obese people in the world (1.5 billion) than there were hungry people (925 million).[13]

9. Suicide is the UK's number-one killer of men under the age of forty.[14]

10. Between 1992 and 2005, armed conflicts around the world decreased by more than 40 per cent and the number of deadly wars fell by 80 per cent.[15]

12 http://www.hsrgroup.org/human-security-reports/2005/overview.aspx
13 http://www.ifrc.org/news-and-media/opinions-and-positions/opinion-pieces/2011/a-world-of-hunger-amid-plenty/
14 According to Christian Vision for Men
15 http://www.hsrgroup.org/docs/Publications/HSR20092010/20092010HumanSecurityReport-Part3-TrendsInHumanInsecurity.pdf

What's wrong with the world?

When *The Times* invited several eminent authors to write an essay on the theme "What's wrong with the world?", G. K. Chesterton's took the form of a letter:[16]

Dear Sirs,

I am.

Sincerely Yours,
G. K. Chesterton

16 Wikipedia

THE JACKBOOT OF INVASION

The jackboot of invasion,
the execution squad;
barbarous acts committed –
some in the name of God.

Despicable achievements,
an iron-hand glossary,
a census of oppression,
a foul inventory.

The nails of crucifixion,
phosphorus bombs and drones,
leg irons and machetes,
the martyrdom of bones.

The aid supply embezzled,
calamity increased,
the looting of the perished,
the maiming of the least.

These journals of maltreatment
transcribed with grieving pen,
of suffering on suffering...
caused by...
the moods of men.

STEWART HENDERSON

Andy's story...

When I was about twenty I walked into work and after the usual pleasantries my boss asked me to sit down for a moment. I wondered what was going on, and then she gently told me that they'd just been informed my best friend had been killed in a motorcycle accident. During the following days of dealing with the shock and pain, if you'd talked to me about suffering and God I probably would have hit you. And I guess that's the hard thing about the question of suffering: if you're in the middle of pain, whether it be physical or emotional, there's not much that can be said that satisfies.

I really was dazed and confused at the time but I remember a couple of weeks afterwards I found myself walking through a park surrounded by people getting on with their lives. Kids were playing and laughing and I felt myself snap back into reality, and in that instant I also felt a new sense of peace. I'd been a Christian for most of my teenage years and, while I wouldn't say I heard God speak audibly, I did get a real impression of something profound which has stayed with me to this day. It was simply that I *would* see my friend again. It was more than a sense; actually it was an absolute certainty. He'd been a Christian too, and though I knew that I'd have to go through life without him, which would always be sad, I also knew that one day we would see each other again.

The interesting thing about this certainty is that it never explained (and still hasn't) why a good, strong, kind young man should be killed in a senseless accident. But nevertheless the peace was there, a profoundly deep peace, and I felt I could wait for an explanation – a wait that would probably last a lifetime. I could so easily have remained angry, and carried a kind of bitterness around, but it just didn't work out that way.

A similar thing happened only a few years back. My father was in hospital for a routine hip replacement operation, and it all went wrong – a real botched job. He didn't die but he did end up crippled for life, unable to walk properly ever again. The dreams of kicking a football with the grandchildren would always remain just that. When I heard, I was livid.

I remember I was driving along with a sense of fury after hearing the news. Again, he was a good man who only helped others. He didn't deserve this. Plenty of people have the same operation, some good people, some scoundrels, and it wasn't fair that my father was crippled. I wanted to drive to the hospital there and then and have it out with the surgeon. To be honest, I wanted to hit somebody responsible. And then I felt the peace again. It wasn't like I was praying and getting myself into some kind of meditative state – forgiveness and understanding were the last things on my mind. But this peace just fell over me like a blanket and I knew God was with me and that it was going to be OK. Again, there was no explanation for why this had happened; just a sense that it was going to be all right.

And it has been. Years on, my father is still crippled, but he's also happier than he has ever been. I don't understand the ways of God, but I am learning to trust that he is good. That doesn't mean I think that people who trust him always come up trumps.

A friend of mine lost one son to suicide and almost lost another to illness. She says something really wise when you speak to her: "God is God and life is life." I think she means that bad stuff happens but it doesn't stop God being good. I know there are a lot of theological words that explain this more deeply, but what she says is good enough for me, because I've experienced the truth of this myself.

Whether it is the tragic loss due to a flood or that of a devastating earthquake, pain is everywhere. It's the way of the world. But I also see that God is everywhere too, and his love and peace can be found in the midst of the pain, and I guess what I am learning is that finding it may mean letting go of anger, blame, and recrimination.

Easier said than done!

Dear God

Have you ever considered letting God know what you think about what is going on in the world?

```
Dear God




Yours sincerely
Me
```

Spiritual exercises

1. It is worth reading *The Hiding Place* by Corrie Ten Boom (Hodder & Stoughton, 1971). The story of two brave women who help Jews in Nazi-occupied Holland, it has also been made into a film.

2. Take some time to think through difficult situations that you have gone through. What can you learn from those experiences?

3. Edvard Munch is well known for his painting *The Scream*. If possible, find the image online and spend some time reflecting on it and what it has to say about suffering.

4. Read in the Bible the account of Jesus' death in John's Gospel (chapters 18, 19, and 20).

Rummaging around in the Bible: Psalm 23

Psalm 23 is probably one of the best-known and best-loved passages in the Bible. In the psalm its author, David, illustrates how the God he worships is involved in his daily life.

Painting several life pictures for us, David makes us aware that wherever we are in life and whatever is going on, God is to be found – wanting to be involved in the here and now and walking with us through whatever circumstances we find ourselves in.

For many people Psalm 23 has been a source of enormous comfort as they have gone through difficult times.

Psalm 23 A psalm of David

The Lord is my shepherd, I shall not be in want.
He makes me lie down in green pastures,
he leads me beside quiet waters,
he restores my soul.
He guides me in paths of righteousness
for his name's sake.

Even though I walk
through the valley of the shadow of death,
I will fear no evil,
for you are with me;
your rod and your staff,
they comfort me.

You prepare a table before me
in the presence of my enemies.
You anoint my head with oil;
my cup overflows.

Surely goodness and love will follow me
all the days of my life,
and I will dwell in the house of the Lord
for ever.

Q. *Where is God when we go through difficult times?*

That's interesting!

In reading through the spiritual songs of David (called the Psalms in the Bible) it seems that God is more than happy for us to challenge and confront him over the injustices that we see.

Holocaust survivor Corrie Ten Boon once said "No pit is so deep that the love of Jesus isn't deeper."

DAY 29

Journal...personal reactions to spiritual matters

What's on your mind... observations, reflections, insights, prayers, words of others, surprises, questions, trials, yearnings, and things to be thankful for.

_____

_____

_____

_____

Stuff to mull over – take a look at the passage for the week, which is **Psalm 23** (page 102), and ask yourself the following: What does the passage say about God, me, others, the world I live in, life... anything else?

_____

_____

_____

_____

God talk – time to talk to God about what you have read and written or to read the Lord's Prayer. Try to say it over your day. Is there anything you particularly want to say to God?

_____

_____

_____

_____

DAY 30
Journal...personal reactions to spiritual matters

What's on your mind... observations, reflections, insights, prayers, words of others, surprises, questions, trials, yearnings, and things to be thankful for.

_____

_____

_____

_____

Stuff to mull over – take a look at the passage for the week, which is **Psalm 23**, and ask yourself the following: What does the passage say about God, me, others, the world I live in, life... anything else?

_____

_____

_____

_____

God talk – time to talk to God about what you have read and written or to read the Lord's Prayer. Try to say it over your day. Is there anything you particularly want to say to God?

_____

_____

_____

_____

DAY 31

Journal...personal reactions to spiritual matters

What's on your mind... observations, reflections, insights, prayers, words of others, surprises, questions, trials, yearnings, and things to be thankful for.

_____

_____

_____

_____

Stuff to mull over – take a look at the passage for the week, which is **Psalm 23**, and ask yourself the following: What does the passage say about God, me, others, the world I live in, life... anything else?

_____

_____

_____

_____

God talk – time to talk to God about what you have read and written or to read the Lord's Prayer. Try to say it over your day. Is there anything you particularly want to say to God?

_____

_____

_____

_____

DAY 32
Journal...personal reactions to spiritual matters

What's on your mind... observations, reflections, insights, prayers, words of others, surprises, questions, trials, yearnings, and things to be thankful for.

_____

_____

_____

_____

Stuff to mull over – take a look at the passage for the week, which is **Psalm 23**, and ask yourself the following: What does the passage say about God, me, others, the world I live in, life... anything else?

_____

_____

_____

_____

God talk – time to talk to God about what you have read and written or to read the Lord's Prayer. Try to say it over your day. Is there anything you particularly want to say to God?

_____

_____

_____

_____

DAY 33
Journal...personal reactions to spiritual matters

What's on your mind... observations, reflections, insights, prayers, words of others, surprises, questions, trials, yearnings, and things to be thankful for.

Stuff to mull over – take a look at the passage for the week, which is **Psalm 23**, and ask yourself the following: What does the passage say about God, me, others, the world I live in, life... anything else?

God talk – time to talk to God about what you have read and written or to read the Lord's Prayer. Try to say it over your day. Is there anything you particularly want to say to God?

DAY 34
Journal...personal reactions to spiritual matters

What's on your mind... observations, reflections, insights, prayers, words of others, surprises, questions, trials, yearnings, and things to be thankful for.

Stuff to mull over – take a look at the passage for the week, which is **Psalm 23**, and ask yourself the following : What does the passage say about God, me, others, the world I live in, life... anything else?

God talk – time to talk to God about what you have read and written or to read the Lord's Prayer. Try to say it over your day. Is there anything you particularly want to say to God?

DAY 35
Journal...personal reactions to spiritual matters

What's on your mind... observations, reflections, insights, prayers, words of others, surprises, questions, trials, yearnings, and things to be thankful for.

_____

_____

_____

_____

Stuff to mull over – take a look at the passage for the week, which is **Psalm 23**, and ask yourself the following: What does the passage say about God, me, others, the world I live in, life... anything else?

_____

_____

_____

_____

God talk – time to talk to God about what you have read and written or to read the Lord's Prayer. Try to say it over your day. Is there anything you particularly want to say to God?

_____

_____

_____

_____

Session 6:
What is the spiritual world and how does it impact my life?

Introduction

In the film *Contact*, starring Jodie Foster, we are introduced to an astronomer who has a mind-blowing out-of-body experience that changes for ever how she will see the world in which she lives.[17] She begins her journey as a scientist whose understanding of the universe is determined by what her hands, eyes, and mind tell her is real. Her grasp of what is out there has been formed by the scholarly books she has read, the numerous experiments she has conducted, and the hours she has spent staring out into space through the many giant telescopes she has worked with.

And then she goes on a space flight that changes everything. The flight lasts only forty seconds but to her it feels like hours. It is while on this journey that she travels to a world beyond her imagination. A mystical world that is overwhelmingly beautiful. A dimension in which she is able to spend some time with the spirit of her father.

As a result of this mystical journey, her understanding of the universe is transformed. No longer understood purely by what she can see, touch or reason, her reality is now also determined by what she has experienced. For Foster's character there is now a mystical or spiritual element to life that is as real as the physical one. Today, many people hold a similar perspective on reality to that of Foster's character after her out-of-body experience. They have concluded that there is a spiritual reality as well as a physical one.

Statisticians inform us that seven out of ten people in the UK and USA pray. When our prayers are answered positively, should we see this as just coincidence, or wishful thinking, or power in

17 Directed by Robert Zemeckis, 1997.

speaking out what we determine to see happen? Or is it evidence of a world that cannot be seen, changing for the better the world that we live in when we cry out to the powers of that world to help us?

Discussion questions

Is spirituality back in vogue?

What's the difference between being religious and being spiritual?

What fills you with awe?

When and where do you feel spiritual?

Have you ever had a spiritual experience? What happened?

What is the spiritual world?

Many people try lots of different faith systems on their spiritual journey. If that is you, what have you learned about the spiritual life?

In the Bible Jesus is presented as someone concerned about radical justice and as having a spiritual presence about him. What's your impression of Jesus?

In your opinion, what differences occur as a result of engaging with the spiritual realm?

What are the characteristics of a spiritual person?

Do you pray? Why? What do you pray about? Does it work?

In what ways can someone connect with God?

Graffiti – What is the spiritual world and how does it impact my life?

"The God Gene" – D. H. HAMER[18]

18 Published by *Doubleday*, 2004.

"We need to find God, and he cannot be found in noise and restlessness. God is the friend of silence." – MOTHER TERESA

"The spiritual life does not remove us from the world but leads us deeper into it." – HENRI J. M. NOUWEN

"Faith is... the evidence of things not seen. – HEBREWS 11:1 (KJV)

"God can dream a bigger dream for you than you can dream for yourself, and your role on earth is to attach yourself to that divine force and let yourself be released to it." – OPRAH WINFREY[19]

19 From the September 2001 issue of O, The Oprah Magazine.

"REMEMBER THAT EVERYTHING HAS GOD'S FINGERPRINTS ON IT."

"God answers all our prayers. Sometimes the answer is yes. Sometimes the answer is no. Sometimes the answer is you've got to be kidding!" – JIMMY CARTER

"No eye has seen, no ear has heard, no mind has conceived what God has prepared for those who love him. – 1 CORINTHIANS 2:9

The land that breaks beyond our dreams

The land that breaks beyond our dreams
has crocuses that do not dip
below the earth of winter.

The land that breaks beyond our dreams
is where the drained begin to leap,
and the faint rustle of the butterfly's wing
is enough to calm you there,
tame with yourself,
and washed of all your woes.

The land that breaks beyond our dreams
is where the glory comes beside us
and surging shoals of daffodils
surf across an ocean
of roaming rainbows.

For –
that will be when
there is no more proud;
and the missing,
the mad,
and the cowed
will know how to sing descant
with the Voice behind the nightingale.

STEWART HENDERSON

Celebration

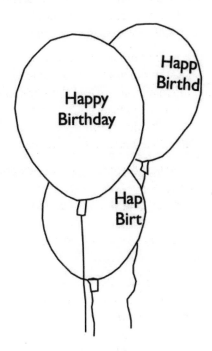

In writing the book of Ecclesiastes, Solomon encouraged his readership to "always be dressed in white". What he meant by that was that we should go through life with our party clothes on.

Organize a party with some friends to celebrate life!

Tendai's story...

How do I connect with God? Well, since God is a spiritual being, it is kind of difficult to connect with someone you can't see.

For me, what I have found helpful is reading the Bible. In that way I find that I can hear God speaking to me about different issues in life.

Also, because I feel that my connection with God is like having a relationship with someone, it is a two-way communication. It is not just about reading the Bible and having God speaking to me; it is also about me speaking to him.

For me, prayer is when I talk to God. So I spend time praying and talking to God about different things that I am facing in life, like the squabbles I have with my wife or the problems I am having with my teenagers.

When I pray I am aware of the fact that God is listening to me. What often happens next is that I will read the Bible and God will speak to me about what is happening and I will be able to figure out how best to respond to those problems.

As far as what difference God is making in my own life...

I find that as a human being, as a bloke, as an individual, I have flaws. I make mistakes; I am judgmental and very critical. I have opinions and I'm stubborn.

God makes a difference in these situations: for example, after I have had a row with my wife and I walk off, I feel an inner tug that I think comes from God, which encourages me to go back and talk to her and work things out properly.

This tug challenges my attitude and pride.

Quite often God provides me with wisdom and guidance to tackle these things and the many other difficult situations that I face.

What is more, when I need comforting I find that God draws near to me. Sometimes I can feel lonely and I sense that God is with me.

One of my favourite spiritual disciplines, which has really helped me connect with God, is making time to go for walks and in particular forest walks. When out walking I talk to God and in doing that I find that he makes a real difference in various ways to what is going on in my life.

Spiritual exercises

1. Borrow a Christian worship CD and spend some time this week listening to it.

2. Over the week, spend a few moments each day asking God to get involved in the lives of those around you – colleagues, family, neighbours.

3. Arrange to meet with someone on a similar spiritual journey to yours and talk with them about what is going on.

4. Keep reading the Lord's Prayer during the week and mull over what you read whenever you get an opportunity.

5. Organize a party.

Rummaging around in the Bible: Luke 11:1–13

In Luke 11 verses 1–13 Jesus talks with his disciples about the role of prayer in a person's life.

He is keen to point out that prayer works. We might not always get the answer that we want, but God will always answer our prayer with the right answer.

Wanting his disciples to have an idea of what to pray about, Jesus teaches them what has become known as the Lord's Prayer, and then tells them some stories that will encourage them to keep praying until their prayer is answered.

We explore the Lord's Prayer later, in our section on how to pray.

Luke 11:1–13

One day Jesus was praying in a certain place. When he finished, one of his disciples said to him, "Lord, teach us to pray, just as John taught his disciples."

He said to them, "When you pray, say:

"'Father,
hallowed be your name,
your kingdom come.

Give us each day our daily bread.
Forgive us our sins,
for we also forgive everyone who sins against us.
And lead us not into temptation.'"

Then Jesus said to them, "Suppose you have a friend, and you go to him at midnight and say, 'Friend, lend me three loaves of bread; a friend of mine on a journey has come to me, and I have nothing to set before him.' And suppose the one inside answers, 'Don't bother me. The door is already locked, and my children and I are in bed. I can't get up and give you anything.' I tell you, even though he will not get up and give you the bread because of friendship, yet because of your shameless audacity he will surely get up and give you as much as you need.

"So I say to you: Ask and it will be given to you; seek and you will find; knock and the door will be opened to you. For everyone who asks receives; those who seek find; and to those who knock, the door will be opened.

"Which of you fathers, if your son asks for a fish, will give him a snake instead? Or if he asks for an egg, will give him a scorpion? If you then, though you are evil, know how to give good gifts to your children, how much more will your Father in heaven give the Holy Spirit to those who ask him!"

Q. What does Jesus teach the disciples about prayer?

That's interesting!

For the writers of the Bible there are parallel worlds: the spiritual realm is as real as the physical one and continually interacts with it.

"Some of God's greatest gifts are unanswered prayers."
(Anonymous)

DAY 36
Journal... personal reactions to spiritual matters

What's on your mind... observations, reflections, insights, prayers, words of others, surprises, questions, trials, yearnings, and things to be thankful for.

_____

_____

_____

_____

Stuff to mull over – take a look at the passage for the week, which is **Luke 11:1–13** (pages 120–21), and ask yourself the following: What does the passage say about God, me, others, the world I live in, life... anything else?

_____

_____

_____

_____

God talk – time to talk to God about what you have read and written or to read the Lord's Prayer. Try to say it over your day. Is there anything you particularly want to say to God?

_____

_____

_____

_____

DAY 37
Journal... personal reactions to spiritual matters

What's on your mind... observations, reflections, insights, prayers, words of others, surprises, questions, trials, yearnings, and things to be thankful for.

Stuff to mull over – take a look at the passage for the week, which is **Luke 11:1–13**, and ask yourself the following: What does the passage say about God, me, others, the world I live in, life... anything else?

God talk – time to talk to God about what you have read and written or to read the Lord's Prayer. Try to say it over your day. Is there anything you particularly want to say to God?

DAY 38
Journal... personal reactions to spiritual matters

What's on your mind... observations, reflections, insights, prayers, words of others, surprises, questions, trials, yearnings, and things to be thankful for.

_____

_____

_____

_____

Stuff to mull over – take a look at the passage for the week, which is **Luke 11:1–13**, and ask yourself the following: What does the passage say about God, me, others, the world I live in, life... anything else?

_____

_____

_____

_____

God talk – time to talk to God about what you have read and written or to read the Lord's Prayer. Try to say it over your day. Is there anything you particularly want to say to God?

_____

_____

_____

_____

DAY 39
Journal... personal reactions to spiritual matters

What's on your mind... observations, reflections, insights, prayers, words of others, surprises, questions, trials, yearnings, and things to be thankful for.

_____

_____

_____

_____

Stuff to mull over – take a look at the passage for the week, which is **Luke 11:1–13**, and ask yourself the following: What does the passage say about God, me, others, the world I live in, life... anything else?

_____

_____

_____

_____

God talk – time to talk to God about what you have read and written or to read the Lord's Prayer. Try to say it over your day. Is there anything you particularly want to say to God?

_____

_____

_____

_____

DAY 40
Journal... personal reactions to spiritual matters

What's on your mind... observations, reflections, insights, prayers, words of others, surprises, questions, trials, yearnings, and things to be thankful for.

_____

_____

_____

_____

Stuff to mull over – take a look at the passage for the week, which is **Luke 11:1–13**, and ask yourself the following: What does the passage say about God, me, others, the world I live in, life... anything else?

_____

_____

_____

_____

God talk – time to talk to God about what you have read and written or to read the Lord's Prayer. Try to say it over your day. Is there anything you particularly want to say to God?

_____

_____

_____

_____

DAY 41
Journal... personal reactions to spiritual matters

What's on your mind... observations, reflections, insights, prayers, words of others, surprises, questions, trials, yearnings, and things to be thankful for.

Stuff to mull over – take a look at the passage for the week, which is **Luke 11:1–13**, and ask yourself the following: What does the passage say about God, me, others, the world I live in, life... anything else?

God talk – time to talk to God about what you have read and written or to read the Lord's Prayer. Try to say it over your day. Is there anything you particularly want to say to God?

DAY 42
Journal... personal reactions to spiritual matters

What's on your mind... observations, reflections, insights, prayers, words of others, surprises, questions, trials, yearnings, and things to be thankful for.

Stuff to mull over – take a look at the passage for the week, which is **Luke 11:1–13**, and ask yourself the following: What does the passage say about God, me, others, the world I live in, life... anything else?

God talk – time to talk to God about what you have read and written or to read the Lord's Prayer. Try to say it over your day. Is there anything you particularly want to say to God?

Spiritual disciplines

Spiritual disciplines act as companions during life's journey. They all have the potential to help us reconnect with the spirit life that is outside ourselves. They can be welcomed as forms of training that help us to observe and practise our spiritual life. As with learning any new skill, they can seem rather awkward and a little strange at first, but gradually, like a new hairstyle or a pair of rugby boots, everything finally sits comfortably.

They enable us to make space for the divine spark that burns in our life. Many of us have very busy lives, so any awareness of the spiritual reality that is all around us is quickly lost as we think about getting the children ready for school, going to work, getting through all the points on our to-do list, attending meetings, travelling home, eating, and trying to catch up with family. But spiritual disciplines, if carefully and regularly scheduled into our week, give us the option of obtaining spiritual refreshment.

Dallas Willard divides his list of spiritual disciplines into two groups: those he labels as "disciplines of abstinence", which he believes refine the drives of the body that may crowd out any searching after the spiritual, and "disciplines of engagement", which aim to bring something of the divine back into our most sacred place. In his abstinence group he includes solitude, silence, fasting, frugality, and sacrifice. In the engaging group he includes study, worship, celebration, service, prayer, confession, and submission.[20]

The actual list of possible disciplines that you can try out as you seek to develop your spiritual life is endless. It's worth looking at a few in a little more detail. For those wanting to get on and have a go, we suggest that you gradually work through the list, picking a couple at a time. Some are going to be fun and some are not (depending

---

20 In his *The Spirit of the Disciplines*, London: HarperCollins, 1991, pp. 159 and 175.

on temperament); some are easy to access and others are painfully difficult. Once you've given all a try, or at least thought about doing them all, you will be in a place to focus on those that suit you.

Prayer

It seems that a great number of people pray already. It is reported that seven out of ten Americans pray on a daily basis, and a similar number in the UK. The core of prayer is the idea of a spiritual conversation taking place between us and God. Depending on the closeness of our relationship with him, we either talk to him as one of his creation or as a child to a parent.

As in all mature conversations, prayer is a matter not only of us speaking to God but also of taking time to listen for him speaking to us. The ways through which he does that could include life's unfolding events, the comments of friends or an internal sense of what is right. Those from the Christian tradition would also want to include what we discover as we read the Bible.

Try taking a few minutes (to begin with) at the start and end of each day, or any other time you find easier for you, and dedicate that time on a regular basis to talk to God. This can be followed by spontaneously mentioning things to God that come up during the day.

In the book *The 8 Secrets of Happiness* the authors identify how many people find it helpful to have a simple blessing prayer that they say before they enjoy something special, such as a meal or a concert or some time with special friends. An example of this type of prayer would be, "Thank you, God, for the gift of... food, friendship... this opportunity... to be able to watch this film or play." Many have found it useful to learn the Lord's Prayer (which we look at later) and recite it at the start of each day. We can use it as a launch pad to pray for other things.

When it comes to what to include in your prayers, anything goes. You can talk to God about your day, and mention things that concern you about your family, friends or work. If after watching the news on TV you are concerned about some political situation in this country or somewhere else in the world, then you can talk to God about that.

It's important to know that prayer is not something that you just do on your knees or in a church on a Sunday, and that when it comes to answering prayer God answers every single prayer that we pray, though (wisely!) not always with a yes.

Meditation

In the Christian tradition meditation is not about emptying your mind but rather filling it with thoughts about spiritual truth as found in its sacred text, the Bible. Rather than attempting to detach our minds from our circumstances, this meditative practice is about exploring the meaning of the text and applying it to the situation that we find ourselves in.

With its motivation being to feed our soul, the aim of this type of meditation is to listen to God speak to us through his word. To meditate means to chew the cud – to put it through the washing machine of your mind and draw from it the life it contains; to turn it over in your mind again and again. As for how to meditate, this is best learned on the job. The skill is to focus your attention, which really only comes with practice. However, some pointers are useful for those starting out.

If it is possible to memorize the section that you are thinking about, all the better, as this facilitates the option of returning to your thoughts again and again throughout the day. If you are able to remember particular passages then you can play with them in your mind in all sorts of locations.

Any meditation should be enveloped by a short prayer for help with the process and then thanks for insights gained afterwards. It is helpful to find a comfortable place that is as free as possible from distractions. In many senses posture is a personal preference, but many people find sitting comfortably with a straight back, with their eyes closed, gently breathing in and out, helps.

Once a sense of stillness has been achieved, the idea then is to use your mind to understand the text. This includes questioning what is there: imagining what it would have been like to be there, perhaps thinking about how that would work out in your life. There is no doubt that your mind will wander again and again from what you are trying to do. When that happens, gently draw your attention back to the task in hand. We are aiming to engage in an unhurried act of thoughtful reflection on a spiritual text. In a world of busyness that is going to be a challenge.

If this exercise simply isn't you, what about taking the text, writing it in the centre of a piece of paper and, after enveloping the exercise with prayer (as noted above), picking up a pen and doodling on the subject of what the text might mean and how it could be relevant for you?

Retreats

It takes most people a little while to appreciate the benefit of taking time out to go on retreat. With such busy lives we often feel that we don't have enough time to stop what we are doing and take time off to go in search of God. At its most basic level, a retreat is carving out in your diary a period of time when you step out of your normal routine, physically move to a different location, and spend a period of quality time seeking after God.

For some people, a retreat takes place in their garden or at a local park or on a favourite walk; for others, it takes place in one of the retreat houses that are found in many countries across the world.

Finding a soul friend

A soul friend is like having your own spiritual guide as a friend. It's an individual who walks with you through your spiritual journey. This is the person you can talk to about how you are getting on in your spiritual journey, issues that you are struggling with, or successes that you are enjoying. Depending on the nature of the relationship, they may be able to suggest ways in which you could move forward in your journey, books to read or disciplines to try. During a difficult period you could ask them to hold you accountable for your actions.

It's important to think carefully about the person you want to be your soul friend or mentor. What qualities are you looking for? What is it about their life that attracts you to them?

Laughter

One of the disciplines missing from most lists is that of laughter. It belongs to a stream of spiritual activities that include being joyful, feasting, celebrating, partying, and playfulness. It is the side of the spiritual life that is often neglected because it is seen as being of less value than the more sober disciplines that are most often called to mind.

Solomon commented in his wisdom that there is a time to laugh. He went on to say that one of the ways of living life in the midst of its realities (we are all going to die, life is a game of chance, and evil and insanity reside in the human heart) was that we were to "always be dressed in white" – which was his way of saying that we should always have our party clothes on. Whatever life throws at you, whatever you go through, learn to do internal aerobics – learn to laugh.

Today, the wisdom of Solomon's words is endorsed by the medical profession, which has no problem in listing the numerous benefits of chuckling – reduction in stress hormones, improved circulation, and the exercising of muscles – as one of the proven ways to happiness. As we set about nurturing our soul we should remember that laughter is one of the key components of this.

Nurturing a world view

In his book *Why Don't People Listen?*,[21] Australian psychologist Hugh McKay commented that we all have a particular way of looking at and interacting with the world we live in. Often called a world view, this belief structure gives explanation and meaning to everything that goes on around us. It shapes our value system, our view of suffering, and how we perceive the future.

---

21 Pan MacMillan, 1996.

Many people have never taken the time to sketch out on a piece of paper their outlook on life, still less considered how the spiritual life interacts with this. Redrawing your understanding of the big picture is no easy feat and very careful decisions have to be made on where you go to receive input. Taking fifteen minutes a day to read the Bible or some other spiritual book and then reflecting on what you read is a good way of beginning to think your way into how you could, should or do look at the world.

Service

Some of us are made in such a way that we find it easier to connect with God when we are serving others than when we are in a group chatting about spiritual matters or on our own with a book, saying a prayer, or listening to a spiritual CD. There are a couple of reasons why this might be the case. First, the God who made the earth joins us in our activity and so we sense his nearness and delight. Second, we have learned to meet God in the people we are serving. A strange but incredibly motivating idea that has been around for at least a couple of thousand years is that in caring for others we meet and serve the God who made them.

Being still with God

Modelled in the seventeenth century by the practically minded French monk Brother Lawrence, the idea is to make your spiritual antenna so sensitive that you are able to know and enjoy the presence of God wherever you are. Component parts of this discipline include remembering God throughout the day, learning to still the busyness of your mind and focus on the fact that God is everywhere and therefore where you are right now, admiring him, and stilling your inner being. It may help to choose a single place where you grapple with this discipline and then try another, and so on.

How to read the Bible for yourself

What is the Bible?

The Bible is the sacred book of Jesus' followers. It is a collection of sixty-six smaller books which have been grouped together in the belief that they have all been inspired by God and are useful for helping us understand God and living deeper lives. When reading or listening to the Bible, Christians believe that they are encountering God speaking to them today. The challenge is to figure out what that means in their daily lives.

Over forty authors were involved in writing the Bible over a period of thousands of years. To get the best out of reading the Bible you should start by reading the material that covers the life of Jesus. One of the books that does this is the Gospel of Mark.

What is the best way to read the Bible?

If you start by reading the Gospel of Mark, then the best way to tackle that book is by thinking of it as a novel – read it as a story. Try to read it in one sitting or in big chunks.

As soon as you have read the book through, read it through again. You might be tempted to rush on and read other books in the Bible (and if that is the case then you could try reading Matthew, Luke or John), but ideally go and read the Gospel of Mark again.

After you have read it a couple of times, it would be good to go through the book again but this time marking all the words that Jesus has spoken – you might want to ask yourself the question "What does this mean to me?" as you read it.

Some people find it very beneficial to read one story at a time and to take a few moments to think about it.

Don't think about covering massive amounts of the Bible

Some people are so inspired by what they read in the Bible that they have a go at reading the whole thing. If that works for you then that is fine, but, as we noted above, it is far better (at the beginning of your spiritual journey) to focus on a smaller section and become familiar with that than to rush through the whole Bible.

Think about what you read

If you go with the book of Mark, then as you read it think about what the words of Jesus mean to you.

Many people who read the Bible find it useful to ask themselves some questions about the words that they have read or listened to.

What do these words say about God the Father?

What do these words say about Jesus?

What do these words say about me? (Are there promises or warnings or instructions?)

What do these words say about the world I live in?

Memorize it

As we mentioned in the section on spiritual disciplines, it can be beneficial to take time to memorize small sections of the Bible and mull over those sections at convenient times – for example, when waiting for a bus or while sitting on the Tube or when having your lunch.

Accessing the Bible

It is possible to buy a Bible from many high-street shops or from one of the online retailers. If you have any difficulty in doing this, do let your PQ hosts know. If you would prefer to listen to the Bible being read as opposed to reading it yourself, you can download an audio version of the Bible from iTunes. Also available are iPhone apps of the Bible.

Handle with care!

The Bible is in all probability the most fascinating book that has ever been written. It contains some outrageous promises and devastating warnings. It is a thrilling book that everyone should read at least once.

NB If you decide to read the Gospel of Mark, there is a brief introduction to the book on the Puzzling Questions website: **www.puzzlingquestions.org.uk**

The Lord's Prayer

One day the disciples of Jesus asked him if he would teach them to pray (Luke 11). The outcome of that request was that Jesus taught them a prayer that we now call "the Lord's Prayer", though it should more accurately be referred to as the disciples' prayer.

As you learn to pray the Lord's Prayer it can be something you recite every day over your life and the lives of those you know and love, or be a guide to inspire your own prayers.

What follows is a copy of the Lord's Prayer and some suggestions on how it can inspire your prayers for what is going on in your daily life.

THE LORD'S PRAYER

Jesus encourages us to ask God for the resources we need to get through the day.

Jesus is keen that we should pray that God's name will be honoured. On the surface this might seem like a rather selfish thing to do – to promote your dad's reputation. What we need to be aware of is that as God is honoured, so goodness and rightness flow into our own lives.

When we pray we speak to one who is our heavenly Father. For those who have had a difficult relationship with their earthly dad, it is important to remember that God is a good and loving Father.

Our Father in heaven,

hallowed be your name,

your kingdom come,

your will be done,

on earth as in heaven.

Give us today our daily bread.

Forgive us our sins,

as we forgive those who sin against us.

Lead us not into temptation,

but deliver us from evil.

For the kingdom, the power,

and the glory are yours

now and for ever. Amen.

We ask that the perfect will of God will be worked out in the situations that concern us. Sometimes it might be right to ask God what that will is.

And what is our confidence in praying these prayers? It is that God is not only our Father but also has a kingdom and the power to accomplish his will in our lives.

Jesus is aware that there is a dark side to life and so he highlights the need for us to be delivered from its effects.

There will be situations in the day ahead that could cause us to trip up in our lives, with potentially serious repercussions for us or our loved ones. Jesus encourages us to pray that we would avoid those situations.

One of the most interesting spiritual keys that Jesus highlights in this prayer is that we are forgiven by God in the same way that we forgive others. It is important to take time every day to forgive those who have harmed us in some way. Now admittedly that is easier said than done, and where there has been very serious wrongdoing sometimes it is simply not possible to forgive. We have written about forgiveness in our book *The 8 Secrets of Happiness*.

What next?

We hope you have enjoyed the Puzzling Questions course and that it has been useful to you as you have explored some of life's deeper questions.

You might find that rather than everything now being neatly sewn up, you have even more questions, and that the questions you started with have become more profound.

All of this is quite normal.

For those of you who want to carry on with your spiritual journey, what follows are some suggestions for ways forward:

- Keep in contact with those you have met on the PQ course – both the leaders and other participants.

- Pop along to one of the events organized by those who hosted this course and see what all the fuss is about.

- There are other courses you might find helpful to do. As well as writing Puzzling Questions we have also written the Table-Talk and The 8 Secrets of Happiness courses; these offer you the space to explore the spiritual dimension and how it interacts with your daily life.

- Do visit the PQ website regularly and take a look at the growing number of articles, features, and downloads available. **www.puzzlingquestions.org.uk**

- Consider doing the PQ course again, but this time bring one of your friends along with you!

Thank you for taking the time to attend one of our courses. We do pray that it has been beneficial to you and that as you continue your spiritual journey it might contribute to what happens next.

Answers

Session 1: Guess who?

1. Alastair Campbell
2. Robbie Fowler
3. Desmond Tutu
4. Vivienne Westwood
5. Friedrich Miescher
6. Marshall McLuhan
7. Martin Sheen
8. Catherine Zeta-Jones
9. Emmeline Pankhurst
10. René Descartes

Session 4: Happiness quiz

1. "You Could Be Happy"
2. Pink
3. "Happy Days"[22]
4. Avril Lavigne
5. Bobby McFerrin
6. "Furry Happy Monsters" (R.E.M. and the Muppets)[23]
7. "Happy People"[24]
8. Sister Act 2[25]
9. Being with someone you love
10. Mumble

---

22 © Norman Gimbel and Charles Fox.
23 Music by R.E.M., lyrics by Christopher Cerf, 1991.
24 From R. Kelly's 2004 double album *Happy People/U Saved Me*.
25 1993; director Bill Duke.

Notes

Use this page to jot down what you honestly think, the questions you might have, or anything else that is on your mind.

Other resources

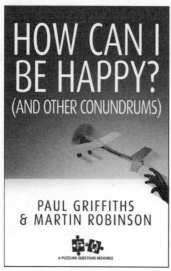

ISBN 978 1 85424 932 6

ISBN 978 0 7459 5329 8